More praise for *The Half-Said Things*

I loved Miriam O'Neal's *The Half-Said Things* for its wondrous questioning and its listening "to the songs a shy girl hears." These are poems grounded in the world where yeasty dough is kneaded in "a red ware bowl the size of a small country." This is a country with a "muffin god" and a "wet wheat ocean," where the speaker is a "fugitive of her own heart." In this place, we enter churches, as well as rooms with cabbage roses on the wallpaper. O'Neal asks, "Whose world is this?/Whose world these?" This collection is a discovery of truths, which can be stark: ". . .only hunger and sea wind/ only song and sway mean/anything." I'll return to this place in *The Half-Said Things* where I am reminded to "Be kind. We are only here so long."
— **Jennifer Martelli**, author of *My Tarantella*

Miriam O'Neal's poems draw one deeply into a bodily experience where all senses are evoked. In the tradition of the great Irish female poet Eavan Boland, who championed the way for women to write poems about their own lives, domesticity, and the landscape within the home, she speaks to the present, to symbol, and to memory through everyday language. There is bread and rain. There are birds and song. A seamstress of words, O'Neal's Irish heritage weaves through this collection as in these beautiful deeply moving lines from her first poem, 'still life with knowledge,' which could also describe her style: *no more than a hum of notes/ from songs her mother's sung/ before, a lullaby about losing love, and though/ she hasn't lost anything yet, she understands.*
— **Attracta Fahy**, Author of *Dinner in the Fields*

The Half-Said Things

MIRIAM O'NEAL

Nixes Mate Books
Allston, Massachusetts

Copyright © 2022 Miriam O'Neal

Book design by d'Entremont
Cover photograph used with permission.

All rights reserved. This book or any portion thereof may not be reproduced or used in any manner whatsoever without the express written permission of the publisher except for the use of brief quotations in a book review or scholarly journal.

ISBN 978-1-949279-41-2

Nixes Mate Books
POBox 1179
Allston, MA 02134
nixesmate.pub

I miss the sky, the weather, the landscape. The soft look. The half-said thing. Where I'm from [ ] the people will say very little and you'll have to find out what happened if you want to know."

– Colm Tóibín (on priests, loss and the half-said thing, an interview with Jenny Mccartney, The Spectator, 24 October 2015)

Contents

still life with knowledge	3
Bread	5
On Viewing Hokusai's, *Under the Wave off Kanagawa*	7
Leaving	8
Practice Sonnet	9
Losing Track of Love	10
Spaces	12
Breakthrough	13
Kinds of Fire	14
The Last Space	15
At the Beach	17
Consider the Ox	19
Natural Law	21
The Kiss Deconstructed	22
Consider the Lilies of the Seine	24
sard bird	25
A Blessing	26
In Trani,	28
This is Serious	29

Prelude	31
Consider the Lilies of the Field	33
The *Wonder Bread* Years	34
Consider the Cormorant	36
All Saints	38
Upon Finding Out You Are Someone You Might Know	41
In the Kitchen	43
Byzantine	45
Green Heron	47
For My Son at Twenty	49
Loving You and Music	50
Repair	52
Getting It	53
Epilogue	55
Church, I	56
Ponies	57
Church, Ostuni	59
Reading Jung in the Morning	61
The Plan	63
Fruit	65
Accent	67

Retrieve	70
Want	72
What It Means	74
The Half-Said Things	75
Remembering Liam	76
Electric Sisters	77
Laughing, Singing Mother	79
For the Record	81
Reign	83
Meditation on Release	85
For My Mother on the 44th Anniversary of Her Death	86
The Charm	88
To the woman in the white sweater who hugged me	89
Little Consecrations	91
Notes	92
Acknowledgments	94

The Half-Said Things

still life with knowledge

she lives in her own shadow, content
to listen to the songs a shy girl hears

when she is good enough to be left alone
while her older siblings sit in school

and the babies sleep, and her mother lays
her exhausted self down on the sofa,

the girl beside her on the floor, and says,
Be good while I just.... light purr of her mother

snoring   soft scratch of yellow crayon filling in
the knotted biscuit of Cinderella's hair,

narrow gash of sunlight falling between
drawn curtains and music in her throat –

no more than a hum of notes
from songs her mother's sung

before, a lullaby about losing love, and though
she hasn't lost anything yet, she understands

what the words mean,
and how it will feel

Bread

There were years when all of our family's bread
came from a red ware bowl the size of a small country.
A yeast user *but scant*, she'd start her dough
on Saturday after the late news for a slow rise.

Then, Sunday, by 7, she had slapped and punched
the airy pillow into 6 loaves and 3 pans of biscuits
and set them on the table for their second coming.
Whichever daughter had gone to the 8 o'clock tasked

with getting the pans in the oven while our mother sang
in Choir at the 10 o'clock and, our Head Usher father
helped the elderly to their pews
and passed the collection basket.

After church, her picture hat with velvet band
and scarlet artificial cherries off at the front door,
she'd check our work, and scold
if scolding was needed.

And if the after-church guests didn't swallow
every one, you might get a pecan sticky bun,
or the caramel in the pan, or the smear
on the serving plate to rub your plain biscuit in.

But my sharpest memories are midnights,
a child insomniac, I'd wander down
to the smell of raw dough and to her bent
over the bowl set on a chair for better purchase,

the wet elastic mass, turned and turned,
tucked into itself, and turned again –
up to her wrists in that wet wheat ocean,
lips slack – hazel eyes gone dreamy,
as if her struggle proved
some ferment of faith –
the light over the table
pouring a halo.

On Viewing Hokusai's, *Under the Wave off Kanagawa*

Hokusai's *Great Wave* fits
into a nine by fourteen frame.

Even so, scale and size are related,
which means the small boats are no match

for what's before them, but their oarsmen must row just the same.
Even if the woodblock print's so small a good thief

could slide it into a largish pocket
or drop it into a spacious purse, the wave

still hurls ferocious foam, the sky still hides
any clear sense of direction,

and the oarsmen must still row the air
as they slide down the trough of the last wave.

Even when the museum lights go out at night
the storm rages.

I imagine Hokusai even imagined that.

Leaving

Clouds stacked on the horizon, like uneven
bales of hay, freak the high-tension lines
into stark relief as I shiver deeper
into my sleeves, head down, hands in pockets.

All day the voices that arrived with my first blood
have shouted admonitions, trying
to make me listen. Like arch angels
they've tried reason,   fear,   then shame.

It's the Feast of the Immaculate Conception
again and a sylph of hope sifts the air
as finely as my mothers fingers
sprinkled flour on the board, enough

to knead the dough. I remember how her arms
absorbed each flip and pummel, her mind
elsewhere.   I know
that when I leave, I won't look back.

Practice Sonnet

I plan to stay in bed this morning,
to practice being quiet and alone,
knowing soon the house will fill again
with sounds of you and the dog tramping in.

How long, I wonder, will my contentment last,
before I wish I could avoid the thrum
of silence in these empty rooms,
and listen for your bird-dog chatter?

How long before the idle croon
of solitude devolves to groaning
like a hole augured at noon in a winter lake
then closes shut in winter's gloaming,

tip-up flag frozen in place – staked
instead of dancing madly at the crappie's take?

Losing Track of Love

everywhere she goes she's a fugitive of her own heart,
                a 45 on a turntable without that little disk
the size of a checker to plug the empty space
        an LP would have filled with music,
                      each song released after a brief *thritch*
of the needle between tracks –

there are no tracks, she's not on a train,
        no vanishing point lies somewhere out ahead, only girls
who thumb messages, the *power-on* light
blinking blue, and a strange stickiness
on her wrist she can't identify
the source of.   Then,   at robins' call

              her rambler mind pushes
the door   open   as she reads

the toad's comma-curve of scat on the flagstone –

              nothing on either side,   as if a blessing
written in the dark

                    by feel has been erased,

all the nocturnal creatures' contributions wiped away –

the voles' italic tracks,   the deer's cup of firm brown periods
            the fireflies' illuminated *Thou and I*,
all that had been written
        by starlight,   by way of night's fancy,   by way
of the sweet dream grief sometimes offers
as comfort for a fraught passage across snowy fields or
            prairies or ocean's churning –

When she awakens, bones journey-weary,
        the sticky wrist's washed clean, the last
comma on the stones' already swept into the long grass
with the night.

Spaces

God is in the space around the form, which is the presence. (Ekhart Tolle)

He lies on the floor at the gym
stretching his hip flexors,
knees drawn up, legs swung left,
one ankle pinned
atop the other.

All morning despair
attempts a form – beheadings
in the desert, refugees
strafed or drowned – the homeless
man who carries his small tank
of oxygen under his arm all over town –
survivor's guilt a heavy, unloaded gun.

Then, here, this Jesus – arms flung
wide, eyes closed over the mystery,
the space between two ribs open,
welcoming the sword.

Breakthrough

I'm hoping that the place I'm breaking through to,
isn't where the lions come to play.

Kinds of Fire

She brings my book to the nursing home
and reads poems to her mother
who has no memories of her own –

It's nice, she says, *They're short
and my mother doesn't have to say anything,
just listen. It seems to make her feel good,*

hearing the words.   I imagine brain cells aflame,
synapses charging like some neuronal Pleiades,
her daughter's voice a struck match
as she reads the line about blue swans
who stir our voices in the blue-black mud
with sunset colored feet.

The Last Space

We imagine painted walls and freshly varnished floors,
the dirt of past lives dug from corners, wiped

from narrow hips of baseboards, the panes picked
clean of too much putty, so light pours in.

We'll make things new in the old way,
by removal – scrape and wash horsehair plaster

until it glows in moonlight. Each chill night
a rat-faced whip-o-will's song frays

our longing, nourishing our loss
of this last, unimproved space.

When we discover where new paint
has dripped and hardened in a drool

you'll abrade the blemish with a knife,
sand it smooth, and I'll feather in the wound

so well only we will ever know
the mistakes that happened in this place.

II

At the Beach

Sunk in shallow water, we waited to exhale.
Our flailing at the sand stirred up a cloud
and sun, piercing the water, lit us like a match –
our small girl bodies paddling like dogs,
parted small waves overhead like a mow
of long grass, our arms streaked with purple fig

and fuzzy stripes. We didn't give a flying fig
that our lungs might burst before we could exhale.
It was enough to sit on the sea floor, the mow
of our fingers like blades cutting the cloud
of sand we'd roiled up. Pawing water the way dogs
dig up a garden for a bone, we flicked the match

tip of the sand flats, lit each other – matched
each others' bars of violet like striped ripe figs,
then burst through sun-split water, left an aquatic after mow
of oxygen, the trail of bubbles as we exhaled
the air from our lungs filling a sonic cloud
when we spoke pretending to be dogs

who knew how to bark underwater, dogs
who, in a grassy field would have snuffled through the mow.
Below the surface we pretended to drink tea, each pursed exhale
from our lips a bubbling garbled match
for some word spoken at the party, *Aren't the figs
especially sweet this time of year. Oh yes, and light as clouds.*

One pinky finger raised, our shell cups stippled in the mow
of water swirled by our commotion, we matched
our parents' party play – nudged elbows, grinned knowingly. And
                                                  when a cloud
threw a shadow cool as chilled green figs
across the bay, we'd surface, spluttering, blow great exhales
and stand to fill our lungs like panting dogs.

In swimsuits sewn to fit like fig leaves, we'd float on clouds,
hold underwater teas, exhale, a pleasure we didn't know would dog
us with longing out of girlhood—mow us down. There is no match.

Consider the Ox

Consider the ox in his stall,
the moon a narrow
gilded wire
against the evening sky.

Consider the great heart
of the ox at rest – lungs
winnowing oxygen
in the warm barn air.

Consider the stones at rest
where the ox hauled them
that morning, stained to a sheen
with September's heavy mist.

The day's work done,
all night the mice will natter
in the loft and fashion valleys
the ox can't wander.

Whose world is this?
Whose world these?
Consider the mud and slough
of grass and gravel a farm is,

the breath and blood and flesh,
metal, leather, tin – pleasure
in the miracle of tamed things.
Consider those who may at any minute be untamed.

Natural Law

A button buck grazes in School House Field.
The school's been gone one hundred years,
and cedars, once replaced by hay, have begun
to reclaim it.

The wild hops in the woods are yellow
now and purple asters frosted brown
from early snow. Night spreads its cloak
and the buck fades to black.

We turn for home as rain begins –
carry the deer, the dark, the cloud crowded sky
with us into the kitchen where lamplight shines
in the water dish and the pilot on the oven clicks.

We leave a trail of mottled rotting leaves from boot
and paw, a bit of wildness. This
is how we live now – these are the rules:
Walk awake. Be Kind. We are only here so long.

The Kiss Deconstructed

My parents' bedroom walls were papered with cabbage
roses. And at each bloom's core, a chocolate drop of an eye
I suspected watched in the dark as they kissed – my mother

with eyes closed, the way she closed them
when they met at the door and kissed each evening,
her lips painted *Cherries Jubilee* – how she closed them

when she stood beside the organ at a funeral
and found and held the last note of some hymn
as an entire congregation faced their grief

or maybe felt the weight of Christ's long body
laid across his mother's in the stained glass of the 13th
Station of the Cross, maybe even grieved the little canticle

of rosy flesh where Mary's wrists disappeared under Jesus,
sun burning through her glass face bent over his, branding
each mourner's cheek with the red gash of her lips.

Once, I watched my father lean into my mother's kiss –
briefcase still in hand, his face still bright with cold,
one arm still caught inside his winter coat where snowflakes

melted one by one like tiny burned out stars,
      There is always the too bent neck,
the draped body, the eyes closed against seeing,

or, as in art Byzantine, someone gazing beyond the frame –
the fine black lines that bind each to the other,
a gesture to where the losses hide.

Consider the Lilies of the Seine

The young people's choir from Paris pours into the coffee shop,
their sunlit faces more a flood of lilies than human beings.

      And as some chant on the satellite radio station drones,
        they open mouths and throats and proffer harmonies –

their tourist maps of Plymouth
rustling like leaves between their fingers.

      One lily with blond hair to her chin accepts
      a deep French kiss from a red-headed lily whose arms

wrap her from behind, whose hands flutter at her ribs.
As she takes his kiss,

      her mandarin lipstick seeps into his lips' crevices.
      The other lilies, dancing around them seem oblivious

to all that stamen- and pistel-ness –
after all, they're lilies from Paris.

      But the unpetalled rest of us? We sigh.
      We sigh and wish.

sard bird

each afternoon as town sleeps
a little bird flits in the shade
of the holm oak

might be the same bird each day
might be a cousin –
same grey back

same chest with rosy stain
flits then sways – has swayed
through Normans and Corsicans,

through Moors –
only hunger and sea wind
only song and sway mean

anything,   she does not know
she is or   that I
am nothing without her

A Blessing

Bless the rotting maple leaves, their wide flat faces
on the concrete sidewalks along River Street.

Bless their splendid tannins steeped
in chill November rains that leave

a thousand perfect leaf stains
my feet pass over.

Bless the oak leaf stains that keep
the maples company – leaves that drifted

close, then stayed all through the storm,
like hands that hold on to a friend in mourning.

Bless the long, split open pods of the catalpas
all over Cliff Street – the rain of acorns,

the shatter of gilded willow leaves
like a carpet unrolled over the curb.

The detritus of all that breathed through summer
and dappled us with shadows gives

this last exhalation as late autumn cold drops in –
gives again –   blessing, blessing, blessing.

In Trani,

a drunk stumbles from the bar into the parking lot
beside the port and proposes to watch our car
for two coins.	My friend offers one

and hours later, recumbent in a folding chair
backed to our trunk, his replacement
proposes he should get the same.

And having just watched the lozenge of the sun
burn a hole in the blue horizon and then drop
like the last bit of a fox's tail into its den

are we going to leave him coinless?
But my friend is firm, the new guard
must collect his share from the man we've already paid.

And with a martyr's sigh our thirsty knight
drags his unfolded chair away,
to guard a pale blue Punto.

This is Serious

The woman at the tall table beside me
asks the small child on his stool,
> *If there was a muffin god would you bow down in worship?*

He's listening but doesn't get her tone
> *(this is serious)*.

So, after asking several times in several ways
she finally delivers the commandment,
> *I am the Lord thy God and thou
> shall not place false gods before me.*

And I think of the cold dead hand of Charlton Heston.

But the boy is stuck on the original idea.
> *If there was a muffin god he'd be my gramma.*

He breaks the shining muffin top off its base and shows
her – *I like this part best.*

In *Plaza de Torors*, Cattafi writes,
The same stars/ as Arabia,   meaning, we share them.

I sip my tea considering those stars –

feel the way Cataffi's lark, in *Moor*, becomes Juliet's

lark exploding morning out of night
wordless god-like –

The teacher turns a page in her *Testament for Children*
but the boy ignores her,

as if the muffin god has silenced her.

Prelude

The dog requires me to linger in the yard
until I hear the birds.
Not birds singing, not birds in flight,
but birds waking in trees – one mentioning
she is hungry, another asking (because he needs to plan)
if it's time to start practicing his bell tone
to signal he's available for mating.

The lady jay with the raspy voice cracks,
Can't you see there are no buds yet on the trees?
And he *scracks* back, because he's disappointed,
Yeah, still winter.   I see.

And their speaking teases at the seam
of light above the hills – their beaks
ripping and tearing at the flannelled night
reveal what night kept kidden –

white trim of farmhouse, shingled barn,
the split rail fence where, yesterday at dusk
a pair of crows played tug-o-war with a linden stick.

The dog nudges my hand to signal he's done
snuffling the tiny cedars in the lawn.
Then, suddenly, starlings drop
by the dozens from the air above the feeder.

More invasion than murmuration, they grab
as much as they can in one go, then scatter
in all directions while the other birds complain

like travelers whose connecting train lies broken
between stations, and sit comparing their agitation
to each other's agitation, then agree it's a terrible system
over all but aren't we lucky?
At least we have this rosy dawn.

And the man-jay, in the green spruce, decides just then,
he's tired of waiting for April and begins to ring
the silver bell of his syrinx.
And the other man-jays can't resist competing.

Consider the Lilies of the Field

Pretend coyotes can talk.
Pretend they happen to meet Jesus
and they ask about the loaves and fishes.
Like, how'd you do that?

Pretend Jesus thinks coyotes are redeemable,
you know, ready for salvation, so he says,
I just believed it.

Pretend the coyotes can't get their heads around that thought –
they're just trying to feed their kids.

The Wonder Bread Years

How does a child manage without wonder?
As soon ask her to live without bread –
without dreams or longing, without a healthy slice
of imagination given free rein – a thought to please
her, like swinging out across the water on a rope,
then dropping where it's deepest in spite of fear.

Because what's the point of swinging if you have no fear?
You can't capture wonder
if you cling tight and swing back to shore, the rope
marking your clenched fists with burns, your loss like bread
so underproved its density pleases
no one, no matter how it's sliced.

If you could release your grip and let the water slice
the heat of summer from your skin, could buck your fear
and rocket through the deepest water in the lake, pleased
to feel your heart race at the wonder
of being the kind of kid whose day was bred
of danger met with daring – the girl who could lasso

all the names the boys had called her and lash
her fear down long enough to let go and slice
the surface with her body – if you could ignore the Sunday bread
that made your mother famous, all that doing good a tale you feared
because you saw the prison there – no wonder,
just a litany of saints and angels to pray to asking, *Please.*

At ten years old the grownups found you pleasing,
but you suspected being pleasing was a rope
wound in a noose to strangle the fun and wander
of running barefoot all through summer – that you might slice
your nose off to spite your face with all that sweetness. Your fear
of being good as bad as your fear of being not good breeding

a shadow that lived inside your shadow, like bread
that came in circus-colored sacks, you were pleased
by its convenience but not its taste, a bread too soft, pasted like fear
to the roof of your mouth, making you wish for a slice
of cold watermelon to help you swallow, or a rope
to swing up and away on, far from the dough

of you about to rise into a girl who always pleases
others. When you think of her you wonder, will she be brave
enough to slice the knot – cast off the rope?

Consider the Cormorant

After three days of rain, Scituate's cliffs
straddle the horizon –
the furthest slash of coastline seeable

from Manomet Point. And I consider
the cormorants, balanced on barnacled shoulders
the low tide has exposed, wings wide open

in a tableau of flight, black backed, chests
tufted white, orange feet spread wide, a streak
of guano trailing behind. Beaks into the wind they know how

to stand as if hanging in the thermals,
red crowns flittering. It's a matter of survival,
this ability to balance on a shat upon rock.

Sometimes life's like that when we're paying
attention. We learn that follow-through takes a while –
that some days it's enough to perch in the light.

It's just, sometimes the weight of water's more
than November's sun can disburse –
we'd like to fly, but know we have to wait.

All Saints

When you stand at the stove
flipping eggs
that Sunday morning,
the sun already above the trees,

I don't know
you will ever not
stand there,
tissue tucked
in the wrist of your sleeve,

your back a long slope
of grey cotton
that grabs your hips
and buckles –

I don't know
you will stand before me
years later, more
than you are at this moment,
because I've lost you –

that you have no idea
who each of us will be
as you hard-cook the yolks.

What this has to do with God
is everything – the believing,
the disappointment,
the having to let go –

how God will drop my hand one day
at a busy intersection,
and I'll cross alone.

III

Upon Finding Out You Are Someone You Might Know

If you find a door in the middle of a woods
you open it, even if it's obvious there's nothing
but more woods on the other side.
You are human – doors help you understand
leaving from and going to.

If you go by way of the road
as far as the place where it bends
and disappears into the woods
you are curious. Roads that disappear appeal.
But if you keep going, you are brave or foolish,
which is the same thing in some languages.

If you hold on to the weight of a dream
after waking, you are hanging across the bow
of a boat that overturned 2 days ago in rough water,
when you should be swimming for shore,
which is close, but you are facing the wrong direction.

You want the boat's promise
that your dream meant something.
You will either sink from that weight
or someone along the beach will haul you in.
A cup of coffee might also do the trick.

If you decide to practice being your true self
you will have to start by being someone
who has lived near a stream in a field.
Each evening you'll lie on your belly in the grass
and watch trout sip damsel flies.

You are not there to catch a fish,
though you know how,
because your true self accepted patience
long ago when you opened a door
in the middle of a woods –
because that you knows waiting is a kind of action
and she doesn't mind the color of the door
which has always caused an itch in this you.

You brush wildflower pollen from your cheek
and notice everything is suddenly familiar.

In the Kitchen

How had I come to be here like them and overhear a cry of pain?
— "In the Waiting Room" by Elizabeth Bishop

Early March. In the kitchen,
my mother stands beside me at the sink

as I try on what to say –
the way I will present my news
as if it were a picture in National Geographic,
some reality we accept just because it is,
like bones pierced through ears and noses
or beetles brimming from the mouths of smiling naked kids.
Without meaning to, our lives shift – make a place for strangeness.

I dry the dishes my mother washes,
her elbows, slick with suds, dimple
and glisten each time she slides a plate into the rack.
The window over the sink's a painting of her face on black
velvet – the kitchen lights buzz.

When I say, *Late*,
the glass in her hand smashes.
As if a poltergeist has flung it at the faucet
it shatters into the silky water.
Bits of corned beef lift off the wreck
of forks and plates – orts of potato drift,
while shards sink like a thousand
tiny hulls of the Titanic.

Late, I say again,
as if reading the caption of a picture
of myself taken next summer.
A ring of blood forms on my mother's wrist.

Byzantine

When Saint Francis cut off Saint Clare's hair
in a gesture of consecration, we might assume
his brothers bore witness to her state of grace,
praying over her small body for her soul.

But in the frescoes by Il Maestro
di Santa Chiara, the men don't watch.
Like a bad family photograph, they look everywhere,
as if a bird had flown in and surprised them
just as the aperture opened, and another bird
called from a branch as it closed.

Even Francis seems distracted.
One hand holding scissors, the other
a hank of Saint Clare's hair, he's looked away.
As I traverse the circle of the crypt, I try
to coalesce that scene into some kind of meditation,

but end each time, with a memory
of the night our neighbor, Carl volunteered

to try to fit our family of fifteen into a single
silver space. Each pop and hiss
of the Nikon's flash a small explosion.

That day the same birds worked the air –
my little brothers bug-eyed in every frame,
and one sister clearly thinking sad thoughts
while the youngest twisted on her toes in holey socks
between our parents whose focus locked

on the middle distance because they couldn't imagine
how to pose with their kids at Christmas.
And in the lower left-hand corner of every proof,
the grainy blur of our blonde lab's wagging tail.

Green Heron

for PJE

Thinking of Pauline this morning –
how, that year, in early Spring

I walked with a friend on the Shining
Sea Path and said, *She's going*

to die. Probably
this year. And I accepted that –

felt the fact
take up residence in my heart.

And we kept on walking.
And a green heron flew by

Its harsh *skeow* accusing us of trespass.

When the phone rang in June,
and my sister, Jane said, *Come*,

I flew at dusk, the space between her hand and mine
a drowsing summer wetland,

her going, in the end, as plain
as a frog slipping off her rock

to glide beneath
the green-black mirror of sky.

For My Son at Twenty

You kiss my cheek goodbye
and in a flash I receive the cinder
of your infant mouth at my breast,
my milk undone.

In late May's twilight
the sugar smell of pink andromeda
drifts through the screens.

Nothing the body knows is lost.

Phantom wing of my own body,
I inhale your sweat and sweetgrass
scent —   burn where your tender scruff
roughs my cheek,   and send you out

to meet the night – God in the loving
and in the tearing from.   At dawn
the honeybees who look too large
still try the heart of each puckered blossom.

Loving You and Music

All morning, the sun undecided and the dog tucked closer
to the wood stove, I wandered these rooms in a reverie
that began with *The Rain in Spain* and ended in *Abilene*.

As kids, we sang and sang and sang.
The answer to every question found in lyrics –
Oh we ain't got a barrel of money,

I'll be taking you home again Kathleen,
If you ever go across the sea to Ireland,
even *Hava Nagila* got its spin.

When I marry again, I marry a musician, and we agree,
for the ceremony we'll find a harpist,
because neither of us knows a thing about them,

so we won't be listening for the unplucked note.
We stand in front of my youngest son's substitute
teacher, whose name is Honey,

and recite our vows like students saying ABCs.
And when she says, *Husband and Wife*, and *You may
kiss the bride*, we're married. And the harpist drags

her fingers across the strings in a flourish as we embrace.
My father finally kisses me on the cheek, but no one sings,
which leaves a cool spot. My mother thought music would save us

from every mean thing. At day's end, as I churn down River Street,
two miles out and returning, the Prime Delivery van passes me
blasting Old Blue Eyes – *My fickle friend, the summer wind.*

Repair

"...what I beheld [ ] astounding darkness. As in winter..." *Dante's Inferno, Canto XXI* (5-6), (Dante goes on to enumerate the practical uses of winter dark, repair oars, ropes, and nets, etc. Those things that labor by summer and daylight wear away.).

All that winter I practiced leaving –
drove to the end of the road,
to the edge of town, all the way
to the state line.

Each time, in my mind I said goodbye –
as if I were never coming back.
But when I packed in spring,
bedding and books, my confusion
curled like a cat across my shoulders,

and drove my old Dodge Dart away
I knew I'd be back – the work of raising
children still before me, the oars of their arms
dipping and swinging through the ocean of my heart.

Getting It

"...we encountered a[ ] troupe of souls/ who looked at us,....///the way tailors do when threading a needle." Dante's Inferno, Canto XV (14-18)

I tried to not want him.
Standing in the elevator of the Buena Vista Hotel,
and earlier, sitting on the couch in the empty lobby.

It was 3AM by then and no one
(by this I mean my husband)
had come to find me.

So, there I was kissing a man I'd just met,
but knew I knew like my own confused
self before it got confused. Get it?

That part of me who had walked her whole life
waiting for someone to agree, words
on paper can change your life.

And hell's waves fell so swiftly in the meeting
of my lips with his, I began my drowning
before we'd reached the 5th floor.

Everyone I thought I knew before then,
said it couldn't be love.
And sinner that I was,

I believed them.

Epilogue

The left foot belongs to the will and drags behind the right foot [which is] governed by the intellect. (Alda Merini)

I could see why leaving would be good
for all involved.
Even my mother would see it.

Church, I

In Trani, the *Church of the Assumption* rises
out of the Adriatic on its wide white pier,
and men pick mussels from the rocks below.

Sometimes they dive for fun and bob, slick-headed
laughing, deltoids rippling as they play. Each black
and blue bivalve in the sack, a pair of angels' wings

the fire will open. Inside the church a fresco
of the Eucharistic blood legend says spilled
in the non-believer's kitchen, converting her.

At dusk rain steams off stone, mixes
with smells of diesel, kelp, and coffee.
Clouds pediment the sun. The steeple cross
glows, gloriously wistful.

Ponies

They trot through a space in the split rail fence, up the yard –
once around a radiant, scarlet quince.   Beau, the lab mutt

scrambles to keep up – sun sheen on everything. On the radio,

a mother says her son's best friend burned to death
when his tank was hit. *They call it a Jack-in-the-box.*

We want our children to come home and live their lives in joy.

At the house on Clifford Road each girl trots across the patio,
her steed in check across the bricks – then drops imagined reins,

and reverts to her real body – a girl in shorts and flip-flops,

mane tugged back in hair-ties, shiny, sweaty neck. The oldest girl
picks up her little sister and old Beau lowers to the grass.

Then, I'm past them, crossing Shingle Brook, but still seeing

the ponies, haunches curved in their steady trot,
the little girl arms' perfect form, elbows close holding reins,

managing the bit so deftly   the pretend horses don't know

they're being guided straight to grandmother's door.
I've seen that form in war footage: the turret gunner's elbows tight

against his ribs as he swings the gun to face his target. The gun,

like a good pony, following his tug. *But how will he find peace
after this?* the mother asks about her own son.

I stare at the radio, then at the river I am crossing. In the rearview

mirror, I see the girls flop on the grass – golden Jerusalem
artichokes towering above their heads and the smallest pony leans

against a bigger sister's chest,   at rest in lengthening shadows.

Church, Ostuni

On the highest hill, above the sea,
the Church of the Annunciation
known for its Bourbon flourishes
and its frescoes of the cousins,
Mary and Elisabeth.

The story goes that when the Allies
began bombing the harbor, the faithful
rushed to the church to sandbag their saints
against concussion, but the less protected
cousin suffered, losing a portion of her arm –
a chunk of her foot, parts of her halo flaked to dust
the priest swept up.

In the dim of candles lit for nickels
to bless the dead, Mary gazes past us
at her cousin's face and upturned wrist,
the open hand that floats without its arm,
the broken foot.

Before the Angel spoke, Elisabeth had already told
Mary her fate – a child, unexpected, loved.
I remember my mother's sister knowing the same
of me – how she watched me from a distance,
silent, smiling.

That night, when the people of Ostuni ran up the hill,
miles overhead each navigator called
longitudes and latitudes to his bomadiers.
As above, so below – in each pair of hands
a crossing   in every mouth, a prayer.

Reading Jung in the Morning

Everything of which I know, but of which I am not at the moment thinking; everything of which I was once conscious but have now forgotton...." Carl Jung

Fire's out,
> flue closed, ashes cold –
>> on the street plows rasp through snow

I had forgotten, words abandon every important thing
> their meanings
unmade beds until spoken
> like the hiss of ashes in the stove
>> stirred in downdraft.

I love Jung for including *all that I cannot remember*, then
> hear the chafe of snow speak your leaving.

That winter on Prospect Street
> pink halogen light spilled on the bed
neither of us very sure, love

a wistful blanket we slept beneath

              I never asked for anything you could give
      or I asked the wrong way
or mis-imagined your answers   I've learned since then

every important thing begins at its end

and now, I wander in dreams
like a lost pet back to its home which it finds empty.

At dawn the ribs of the fire grate a frieze
of white ash   your sleeping face everything

of which I once was conscious.
It was, Love –

The Plan

So, if an angel walks into a coffee shop
looking for me to share God's plan,
I figure, because I'm me
I'll be busy reading or down back
using the loo, and I'll miss the moment

and have to carry on like always,
with the cramped space between
my dog and husband in bed,
and the stickiness of my students'
boredom and/or need
will stay with me too,
while the angel leaves straight through
the plate glass store-front, the way angels do,
or uses the door for the novelty,

but either way, my life will be like it's been
and I'll miss my chance to be a beacon

or a green channel drum showing the way back into harbor
or one of the big red nuns 2 miles out that rolls on the swells
in deep fog, tolling, tolling, tolling,
telling the ships that can only see each other as blips on radar,
Be careful. Follow the chart. Don't cheat.

And I won't get to bellow and bang over my brother's ashes
where we sank them near the shipping channel 7 years ago,
won't be there to call out, *Hello, hello, hello*, say, *We miss you.*

If only the angel would let me know she's coming
and she has a plan in her pocket or under her tongue
like a piece of unchewed communion wafer –
something I imagine angels are allowed to do
without it being a sin – a plan as balanced
as Titian's *Venus of Urbino* or Bruneschelli's church,
or milkweed once it's died and burst,
spilling silks and seeds. I'd be there.

Fruit

I coaxed an avocado tree out of its pit
suspended in a glass on my kitchen sill,
until a thready root worked its way down
and tremulous, a two-leafed stem
yearned up toward daylight.

To induce the birth, I cut the marrow deep
then pierced the seed with toothpicks
to balance it on the glass's rim
in just enough water to urge the kernel
to drink without drowning.

I change the water once a week
and turn the toothpick spokes to keep
the newborn growing straight instead
of crooked as it reaches for sunlight.

I love its being so astute and scrappy
as to know how to be born from a wound
on a windowsill in a cold New England

spring. Of course, it will only grow as large and leafy as the pot I give it.

And it will never give me fruit.

Accent

Someone complains outside of Mullen's Bar,
in a voice that scours the ear of *r*.

A voice that speaks *ciggies* and *beeahs*,
like my brother Paco. Eight years in the Navy

and twenty years down South, the flat *a* held.
The *g* still dropped from every participle with

that minor whine of too tight adenoids,
as if each word were caught in a snare of bones.

I didn't think I'd miss that sound, but its scrape
against my cochlea calls up the glow of streetlights

shining down on small square roofs
of telephone booths where he stood talking

to our mum from Saginaw or Raleigh. And before
that, how he hunched his shoulders, thumb out

trudging Route 3A at midnight, an hour's walk
and 2 rides home, only cigarettes to warm him.

Maybe the sound cuts deep because I saw him peel
wet socks from swollen feet after the late shift,

and sometimes heard the last gulp of beer come back up
in protest, or because, so often, he slept

fully clothed in the den under an afghan until noon,
while we moved noisily around the kitchen.

Maybe no one protected him,
because they didn't know they should,

because a boy in a small town shouldn't need protection
from bigger boys or poisonous men.

Maybe because, as a kid he took hold of life with both hands,
and at 60, every bone fissured by cancer, he refused to let life go –

when I hear that accent, I remember
what's been stirring up lately in dreams,

he's telling me life's what I make it,
grief or no grief.

IV

Retrieve

My husband shuts me in my room.
This happens sometimes.

He's making a narrow space
where our puppy can learn retrieving.

It begins with a pair of socks
curled heel to toe into a sack – tossed

the length of two closed doors
toward a closed window.

Only one person at a time can train a dog
but each can reinforce the good behavior.

I am reading lines from Mary Daly's, **Sin Big**,
Decode their mysteries....

The pup must wait for the command. *Fetch*.
If the trainer delays the pup too long

or berates too harshly interest wanes
and the retrieve will never happen.

When their session's done they go downstairs.
My door's still shut. So I open it.

Want

Last night, we saw the grackles rise
out of the yellowwood,
their clicking all we knew of them

until they rose,
kerned the air above the stubble hay –
curled as waves curl

back from shore across the scruff
of their own seafoam,
sibilant as silk on taffeta –

as when Odette
would rush along a swept stone path
toward a lover,

fed up with Swann's sulking, a copse
of cypresses knifing
the low red sun as autumn's smoke

shot through the weft.
So much depends on happiness.
We watched the flock

break into twos and threes, settle
in the lindens – how
their silence made them disappear.

There will be no child.

What It Means

I take a break from reading Levi-Strauss's *Myth
and Meaning* as dry leaves skitter across the lawn.

The wind's in everything this November morning,
a happy rambunctious child.

Last spring I planted spinach that never grew. And now,
a single seedling's popped open in the stripped bare bed.

The Half-Said Things

Last night, as the breeze died, we felt the stifle
slip through screens. This morning, Jock arrived
to cut the last wildflowers and alfalfa.
Four short turns and done.

The dog has sniffed the after-mow,
nosed the stems, pawed back a swatch to inspect the fragrant stubble
while we sip coffee on the patio.

Words fail. The shade slides
past us. Birch leaves, practicing for cooler weather,
clatter when they kiss. You mention the geese
have flocked. Night and day crickets and katydids

pitch their songs – clocks ticking.
The two fledged osprey have stopped keening
to be fed. We follow the shadows, drag our chairs,
leave tracks across the grass that will be disappear by evening.

Remembering Liam

"He was just walking with time as wind does with the air, in and away."
— Ankit Shah

He was just walking with time as wind does
was walking as wind does with time,
just with the air in deep and away,
walking
with walking, he was just air
time, wind does as he does
as with wind the air does walking,
wind was walking, just as time does,
does he walk with the air away,
with wind in deep and
the time was just as he was
air with wind with away
and in. He was time he was air he was walking
deep and away.

Electric Sisters

for EF, in memory of Becky

I have a memory of your memory –
a mother and two daughters unnested
nesting dolls all facing the same direction,
ash blonde and blue-eyed,
the older girl brushing her little sister's
hair, the mother's brush crackling static
as she brushes out the bigger sister.

Sparks fly.   Both girls jump.
Strands of hair rise to meet the bristles
as if a levitation spell's been cast.

All that winter, the same ritual
as the sun rises.
All day in school, the girls, electric
current running down the hall from one
homeroom to the other. And on the bus
one's hand beside the other's, heads bowed

over magic books as winter's skyline
flashes by in lavish crimson streaks through naked trees.
Home is your sister.

Brushes on the dresser, side by each,
the mother, having combed them clear
reserves a strand or two as keepsakes. This
is the memory that opens as I read your news –

the breath of sisters sweet
as applewood burning.

Laughing, Singing Mother

Most dangerous in movie theaters, in the dark
you couldn't see the elbow coming, and you sat so close
you couldn't get away as she jabbed your ribs to share
her pleasure. And those moments when she just had to
mouth the words to Oklahoma or Big Spender?
Oh my! At least the dark gave cover for the laugh
that lasted longer than the other mothers' laughs. Once back
in the bright-lit lobby, no shame could be attached.

Tuesday night, homework done, we'd watch Red Skelton.
Gertrude and Heathcliff, those loving gulls, made her smile.
She laughed at the philosophizing bar-fly.
Then, Red would sing the closing song and she'd sing along.
No more laughing, just a sweetness measured out in notes
that rang in our ears like little bells –

The time has come to day goodnight, my how the time does fly.
We've had a laugh, perhaps a tear and now we say goodbye.
I really hate to say goodnight, for times like these are few.
I wish you love and happiness in everything you do.

*The time has come to say goodnight, I hope I've made a friend.
And so we'll say, May God Bless you until we meet again.*

Tucked in our beds, sometimes we'd hear her down in the kitchen.
Scrubbing the stove or kneading dough she'd be
chuckling   and humming.

For the Record

She had a sister named Maggie?
How does a Margaret get one of those?
and where are the other siblings I've heard
existed, whose names I don't know?

And how did Ballygar get in there
in place of Tuam or Slievefin?

And what did she do with her own girls
after Patrick died and she went back to being
the maid in other people's houses?

All day the rain flies slantwise.
The wind drags on the chimney smoke
like sailors on their cigarettes after the shelling
stops and their ship still floats.
All day,

I've chased the tail of facts
that won't add up. Born 1897,
maybe 1894? Depends

on which crystal ball of data
you're divining. All day
I've felt her glancing around my rooms,
chamois cloth and damp sponge twitching
in her fingers at the sight of my dust.

I've asked for guidance each time
I pass her tucked among the pictures
of my sons – first great-grands – the ones
she forgave me my divorce for, the ones
I left the church for, emigrating
to the foreign shore of no religion.

I pretend it was our common bond,
that sailing out toward what it takes –
willing to be listed as *scrub woman* in the 1930 census
or to be known as the one who walked away
from the marriage that might kill her.

For the record, we each walked up a gangplank
and sailed –

Reign

I miss the sweet barista with the gentle eyes
who carried my coffee to me as jewels to a queen –
not subservient or humble. Kind.
As if a queen alone on her throne is a sad situation
and coffee might help, his smile touching her.

I miss the taste of a chocolate coronetto
at the kitchen table of my friend,
who notices the queen's distraction,
which will turn out to be her reign
over loneliness, a land which rules me.
When my friend speaks my name I come back to this land.

I miss Mamma's damp hand gripping my arm
as we traverse la scala, her head just above my elbow,
her quavering voice making the opera live,
her firm belief that the queen understands Italian
and the language of the hands.

We must go away to miss things and people.

We must enter a foreign land alone and marry
far away. So I take my missing with me like a parting
gift of roses – their stems covered in thorns,
their intoxicating perfume.

Meditation on Release

for PJE

Lately the dog's long body sprawled
across the bed becomes the great stone
across the tomb's mouth, and my dreams
fill up with hieroglyphs revealed by flames,
and by the high, radiant cheekbones
of my sister's face at Christmas –

the way she washed her chin with skinny fingers,
and her eyes looked everywhere at once,
as if we were one of those illustrations
of the 20 hidden things: *Find the cat, find the elephant,
find the tiger in the grass.*

When the coyotes wake me before first light, I forget
which language I used to speak.

For My Mother on the 44th Anniversary of Her Death

I have a desk
in a room
that's mine.
Space.

I come and go
at will, no one
stops me. I have
space

to make a holy mess
of – and I do
sometimes
space

out and forget what blessings
look like. You
had no
place

to create a world
apart. Your words
sometimes
pace

my mind – come and go
in this room
made by
place

and time and how I chose at last to claim
my own mind   left time
to dream.
Grace

is so easy to lose track of –
turn around –
gone! No
trace.

The Charm

This noon, finches claim the feeder –
muddy scarlet house-, and golds in their winter drab.
They flick away the titmice and juncos
who lurk in the privet, grey on buff
or black on grey, who must dart for seeds
while the finches chaff their fill.

I used to wait for him on my perch, hope he'd choose me,
though I didn't know how a boy decided.
And no one bothered to explain I was unnerving –
my bookishness a charm of words made most boys flounder.
The years have passed and that bird's flown
to wives wedded and left, and fledglings

spun in nests of promises, then discarded. And I,
settled as a stone, unwinged?
What should I do with this happiness?

To the woman in the white sweater who hugged me

I'm sorry I've lost your name, which I asked for in all sincerity.
It was a hectic night – books to sign, friends to greet,
the headiness of applause fresh in my bloodstream.

And there you were, the look in your eyes
telling me something
had happened to you in that room.

Was it the thought of going free like the birds
in my last poem – some childhood memory
shaken from its nest to pirouette in winter flannels?

I'm still thinking of your embrace,
the way you stayed close longer than the others,
shorter than I am, gazing up,

your white sweater, its neckline of ribbon rosebuds
like a pillowcase pinned on a line in winter sunlight.
Thank you, I know I said that at least,

when you leaned against my chest and said, *I loved…*,
but didn't finish. My mother sometimes did the same –
left words unsaid.

Little Consecrations

A plague of grackles
A clutter of starlings
A scold of blue jays
A chirm of finches (any kind)
A rafter of turkeys
A ubiquity of sparrows
An echo of mockingbirds

A drum of goldfinches
A bobbin of robins
A hover of hummingbirds
A charm of house finches
A chime of wrens
A dissimulation of chickadees
A blessing
     a hermitage
          a beatitude
               of bluebirds
                    A sky

Notes

All translations of Dante's Inferno come from Robert Pinksy's translation, Farrar, Strauss, Giroux, 1994

"Laughing, Singing Mother" includes the lyrics of the closing theme song for the **Red Skelton Hour**, which appeared in various formats from 1954 to 1970.

"Loving You and Music" references several songs. Wikipedia tells us the following: Harry McGregor Woods wrote a song called "**Side by Side**" which was popular in the 1950s and sung by everyone from Dean Martin to Brenda Lee to Patsy Kline. The opening line is "Oh we ain't got a barrel of money…"

"If you ever go across the sea to Ireland" is the opening line of the song "**Galway Bay**" which was written by Arthur Colahan in 1947 in Leicester, England made popular among Irish immigrants and/or their descendants in the United States by Bing Crosby.

"**I'll Take You Home Again, Kathleen** " was written by Thomas Paine Westendorf (1848-1923) in 1875. (The music is loosely based on Felix Mendelssohn 's Violin Concerto in E Flat

Minor Opus 64 Second Movement). In spite of its German-American origins, it is widely mistaken to be an Irish ballad.

"Byzantine" references Il Maestro di Santa Chiara, who painted 13 frescoes on the walls of the lower church and crypt in the Basilica of Saint Clare in Assissi. There is some dispute as to who the painter was.

"Epilogue" the epigraph is from Italian poet, Alda Merini's memoir A Rage of Love, translated by Pasquale Verdicchio, Guernica, Toronto/New York 1996

Names for groups of birds vary country by country and even within regions. The names used in "Little Consecrations" were gathered haphazardly and are not guaranteed to be agreed upon by birders and/or ornithologists

Acknowledgments

Thanks to the editors of the following journals for publishing the following.

The Literary Nest: "Remembering Liam"
Nixes Mate Review: "At the Beach"
North Dakota Quarterly: "Byzantine" and "Church, Ostuni"
Poetry Porch: "Consider the Ox," "Consider the Cormorant,"
    "Natural Law"
Princemere Poetry Journal: "Want"
Writing in a Woman's Voice: "The Charm"

Thanks to my wonderful collaborative, The Wild Geraniums (Eileen Cleary, Kelly Dumar, Gloria Monaghan, Christine Jones, Annie Pluto, and Sarah Dickinson Snyder). Your care-filled reading and shared love of the practice has been a joy. Thank you as well to Mary Kane and Barbara Siegel Carlson, who have walked beside me for years, sharing tea and words, and to Dzvinia Orlowsky, who started me down this making of books from my poems path. And enormous thanks to the Editors at Nixes Mate, Michael McInnis and Annie Pluto, for taking such care of the manuscript that became *The Half-Said Things*.

About the Author

Miriam O'Neal is the author of *We Start With What We're Given* (Kelsay Books, 2018) and *The Body Dialogues* (Lily Poetry Review Books, 2020) which was nominated for a Massachusetts Art of the Book Award in 2020. Her poems have appeared in *Blackbird Journal*, *Lily Poetry Review*, *Nixes Mate Review*, *North Dakota Quarterly*, *Solidago Journa*l, and elsewhere. She has been a Massachusetts Cultural Council finalist in poetry and in the Disquiet International Poetry Competition and the Westport International Poetry Competition as well as being a Pushcart nominee. She is the 2020-2022 Plymouth Poet Laureate Runner Up.

42° 19′ 47.9″ N   70° 56′ 43.9″ W

Nixes Mate is a navigational hazard in Boston Harbor used during the colonial period to gibbet and hang pirates and mutineers.

Nixes Mate Books features small-batch artisanal literature, created by writers who use all 26 letters of the alphabet and then some, honing their craft the time-honored way: one line at a time.

nixesmate.pub

www.ingramcontent.com/pod-product-compliance
Lightning Source LLC
Chambersburg PA
CBHW051807100526
44592CB00016B/2597